# Spotted Dogs and Messy Monsters

Ruth Thomson
and Pie Corbett

Chrysalis Education

Distributed in the United States by
Smart Apple Media
1980 Lookout Drive
North Mankato, Minnesota 56003

Copyright © Chrysalis Books Group Plc 2004

The Library of Congress Control Number: 2003116149

ISBN 1-59389-136-9

Editorial manager: Joyce Bentley
Editor: Nicola Edwards
Designers: Rachel Hamdi, Holly Mann
Illustrators: Rebecca Finn, Brenda Haw,
Guy Parker Rees and Liz Pichon

Printed in China

# Contents

# Speaking and listening

Yum, yum, in my tum!

Talking helps children to think, communicate, and make sense of the world around them. Children's speech flourishes where there are interesting activities to discuss. This happens through play, discussing what is happening around them, looking at interesting objects and books and talking about events at home or in school. Recounting what the family or class has done and inventing stories together are helpful ways to develop talk and imagination. Saying funny sentences, inventing rhymes, and singing are also important.

This book is designed for adults (whether parents, carers, or teachers) and children to share together. It is brimming with activities that will give children opportunities to talk out loud, develop their abilities to speak in a wide variety of ways and listen carefully.

## The activities

Each double page has a particular focus (see the contents page) and is completely self-contained. You can open the book at any page, talk together about what you see in the detailed pictures, and go backward or forward at whim.

Although the book has no fixed order, the activities in the first half are easier than those in the second half. The early pages encourage children to talk in simple sentences to describe, match, or categorize people, animals, or objects and to ask questions. Later pages stimulate children to respond at greater length—giving directions, describing a sequence of events, or making up stories.

You do not need to do all the activities on each page at one sitting. The book has been deliberately designed to be re-read again and again, with more things to discover at each re-reading.

## Extension activities

There are further suggestions of things to do related to each theme on pages 30 and 31. These, in turn, may prompt you to invent more activities of your own.

## Talking and listening guidelines

There are suggested guidelines for how good speakers and listeners behave on page 32.

# How to use this book

The four activities at the bottom of each double page provide starting points for conversation. Some invite children to discuss what they see and use talk in an exploratory way. Others require a more formal response, using particular sentences and vocabulary. In some cases, sentence openers or models are given in bold print. These are suggestions for developing different types of sentence or vocabulary, such as comparatives or the use of time connectives (e.g. then, after, next) which will help children develop their talk beyond one or two word comments. You could also lead from a talking session into writing.

The pictures have been drawn so that there are usually many different possible responses as an atmosphere of "getting it right or wrong" will not encourage children to speak. Children talk best when they feel relaxed and the people around them are interested in what they have to say. If children seem uncertain, begin by

modeling a sentence structure (the text preceded by the speech bubble). If a child's reply misses a word or lacks clarity, repeat a clear version.

## Copycat

The children could also play *Copycat*, repeating sentences that you have just said. Use a glove puppet to make this game more fun. Ask a question to which the puppet replies. The children then imitate the puppet. After you have modeled a few replies, the children can think of a reply for themselves, rehearse it in pairs, and say it aloud to the class.

*a list of useful words*

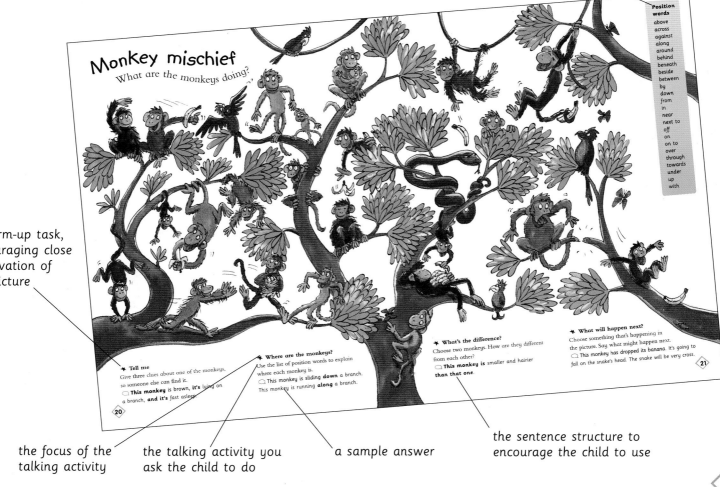

*a warm-up task, encouraging close observation of the picture*

*the focus of the talking activity*

*the talking activity you ask the child to do*

*a sample answer*

*the sentence structure to encourage the child to use*

# Cliffs, sand, and sky

Say the sounds.

**★ Tell me.**

Describe a person in the picture.

💬 **I can see** a girl in spotted shorts and a striped t-shirt, playing with a ball.

**★ Say beginning sounds**

Choose a beginning sound from the panel, e.g. **fl**
How many things can you find that *begin* with that sound?

💬 **fl**ag, **fl**ippers, **fl**oat

**Some beginning sounds**

**br-** (as in **br**ead, **br**ush, **br**idle)
**cl-** (as in **cl**own, **cl**ub, **cl**iff, **cl**oud)
**cr-** (as in **cr**ab, **cr**ane, **cr**ate, **cr**owd)
**dr-** (as in **dr**ess, **dr**um, **dr**ink)
**fl-** (as in **fl**ag, **fl**ippers, **fl**ute)
**gl-** (as in **gl**ass, **gl**ider, **gl**asses)
**gr-** (as in **gr**ass, **gr**apes, **gr**andma)
**pl-** (as in **pl**ate, **pl**um, **pl**ane)
**sp-** (as in **sp**ade, **sp**eedboat, **sp**oon)
**str-** (as in **str**awberries, **str**eamers)
**sw-** (as in **sw**eatshirt, **sw**immer)
**tr-** (as in **tr**ay, **tr**ee, **tr**ousers, **tr**ainers)

**Some end sounds**

**-ck** (as in clo**ck**, ro**ck**, sti**ck**, sa**ck**)
**-ll** (as in ba**ll**, gu**ll**, be**ll**, do**ll**, wa**ll**)
**-mp** (as in ca**mp**, ha**mp**er, pu**mp**)
**-nd** (as in ba**nd**, sa**nd**, ha**nd**)

**Beginning and end sounds**

**-sk-** (as in **sk**y, **sk**irt, kio**sk**, fla**sk**)
**-st-** (as in **st**ar, **st**eps, **st**ilts, ve**st**)

✸ **Say end sounds.**

Choose an end sound from the panel, e.g. **-ck**.
How many things can you find that *end* with
that sound?

◯ sti**ck**, clo**ck**, ro**ck**, sa**ck**

✸ **Match the sounds.**

Choose an object, e.g. **st**eps.
Find another object which starts (or ends)
with the same sound.

◯ **St**ilts start with the same sound as **st**eps.

⬦7⬦

# Colorful characters

Annie

George

Jessica

Sanjay

Alice

Danny

Dave

Susie

Shirly

★ **Tell me**

Describe one of these people, e.g. Susie.
Can someone else guess who it is?

💬 **This person has** curly red hair, green eyes, earrings, and a spotted jumper.

★ **Asking questions**

Ask questions to find out which character someone else has chosen.

💬 Is your character a girl? Does she wear glasses? Is her hair black? Does she have brown eyes?

★ **Say how they match**

Choose two people who have something
in common. Say how they match.

💬 Dave and Jessica both have blue eyes.
Danny and Bob are both wearing hats.

★ **Make the link**

Choose two characters.
Make up a sentence to link them.

💬 Sanjay smiled at Alice.
Alice shouted at Stuart.

# Monsters everywhere!
### Find the monsters.

★ **Tell me**

Talk about what one of the monsters is doing.

💬 **I can see a monster** trying to scare the boy in the bedroom.

★ **Using adjectives**

Describe what one of the monsters looks like.

💬 I can see a **red** monster with **purple stripes** and **spikes down its back**.

**★ Find the hidden monsters**

Find a hidden monster and say where it is hiding.

🗨 A *green* monster is **behind** the curtains in the living room.

**★ Ask a question**

Ask questions about the picture for someone else to answer.

🗨 Why hasn't grandpa noticed the monsters?

# Princess Polly's birthday

## Describe the guests at Polly's party.

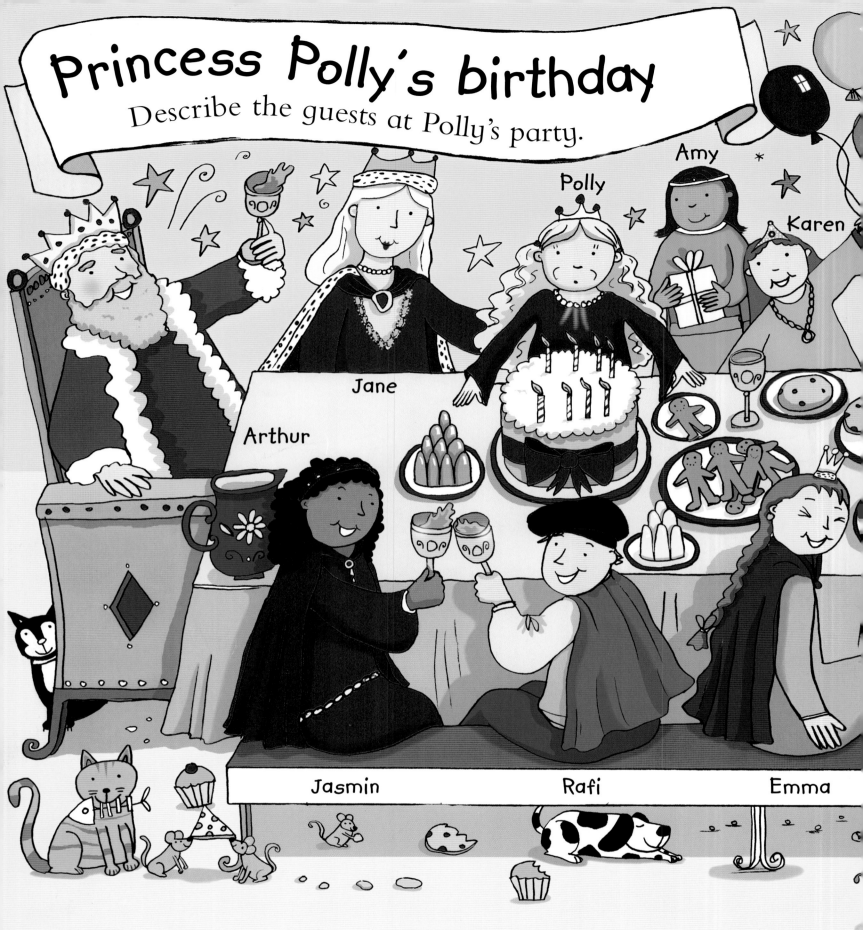

**Tell me**

Give three clues about one of the people, e.g. Princess Polly, for someone else to guess.

🗨 **This person has** curly blonde hair. She is wearing a purple dress and a gold-and-red crown.

**Asking questions**

Ask questions to find out which character someone else has chosen.

🗨 Is this person holding balloons? Is she smiling?

★ **Answering questions**

Ask questions about the picture for someone else to answer.

◯ What is Princess Polly doing?

◯ Why is Princess Emma laughing?

★ **Compare and contrast**

Choose two characters. Say how they are the same or different.

◯ Amy and Flo both have black hair. Amy's hair is short and Flo's hair is curly.

# Mix and match
### Talk about everyday objects.

**✦ Tell me**

Choose an object. Say what you know about it.
What is it? What is it like? How do you use it?
◯ **This is a** spade. **It has** a handle and a metal blade. **You use it for** digging.

**✦ Categorize**

Find four things that have something in common,
e.g. that can cut, hold water, have handles, make a noise, are made of metal. Say why they go together.
◯ The knife, ax, scissors, and saw are used for cutting.

✹ **Compare and contrast**

Pick any two objects, e.g. the scissors and the triangle.
Say what is similar about them and what is different.

◯ **They are both made of metal. Scissors cut.**
**A triangle makes a noise.**

✹ **Make a list**

Choose five things to take to the beach on hot day;
on an expedition to the jungle; into the backyard or
to a cold place. Say why you have chosen them.

◯ **I would take** flippers to the beach for swimming...

# Woof! Woof!
## Spot the dogs.

★ **Tell me**

Choose any dog and describe it.

○ **This dog is** spotted. **It has** short ears, a long tail, a blue collar, and a bone in its mouth.

★ **Listen and look**

Describe a dog for someone else to find.

○ **Can you find** a dog with floppy ears, a short tail, and a red collar?

**★ Pick a pair**

Describe two similar dogs for someone else to find.

◯ **I can see two dogs** with short ears, sitting up to beg. Which are they?

**★ Compare and contrast**

Say how two dogs are the same and different.

◯ **These dogs are both** spotted with long tails.
**One has** a green collar and **the other has** no collar.

# The Glitz Hotel

### What's happening here?

★ **Tell me**

Describe some characters in the first picture.
Say what they are doing.

○ **I can see** three children in a bedroom
on the first floor having a pillow fight.

★ **Ask some questions**

Ask questions about the first picture
for someone else to answer.

○ **What is** the waiter doing? **Who is** fast asleep?
**How many** children are bouncing on the bed?

★ **Compare and contrast**

Compare a room in both pictures.

🗨 **In the first picture**, a woman is reading a book and rocking her baby. **In the second**, the cradle has tipped over and the baby has fallen out.

★ **What might happen next?**

Continue the story of what might happen next to any of the characters.

🗨 The woman might pick up the baby and comfort it. She might take it onto the balcony.

# Monkey mischief
## What are the monkeys doing?

★ **Tell me**

Give three clues about one of the monkeys, so someone else can find it.

○ **This monkey** is brown, **it's** lying on a branch, **and it's** fast asleep.

★ **Where are the monkeys?**

Use the list of position words to explain where each monkey is.

○ This monkey is sliding **down** a branch. This monkey is running **along** a branch.

20

**Position words**

above
across
against
along
around
behind
beneath
beside
between
by
down
from
in
near
next to
off
on
onto
over
through
towards
under
up
with

★ **What's the difference?**

Choose two monkeys. How are they different from each other?

🗨 **This monkey is** smaller and hairier **than that one**.

★ **What will happen next?**

Choose something that's happening in the picture. Say what might happen next.

🗨 This monkey has dropped its banana. It's going to fall on the snake's head. The snake will be very cross.

**21**

# At the park

### Find the way.

Walk

Run

Crawl

Jump

Hop

Skip

Leap

**★ Find the way**

Choose a gate to enter the park. Describe the route from the gate to the café. Say what you pass on the way.

◯ **First I** pass a lady in a green hat. **Next, I...**

**★ Give some directions**

Choose a person and tell him or her how to get to a place in the park.

◯ **To get to** the ice-cream stall, go straight on past the flowerbeds. Carry on past...

**✦ Design an obstacle race**

Invent an obstacle race around the park and tell the children what to do. Use the little pictures to give you some ideas.

🔍 **Hop** along the path towards the bridge.

**✦ Make up some rules**

Some people are spoiling the park. Make up some rules to keep the park clean and safe for everyone.

🔍 Do not drop litter.

Keep dogs on a leash.

# What did you see?
## Who goes there?

### Characters (Who?)

### Objects (What?)

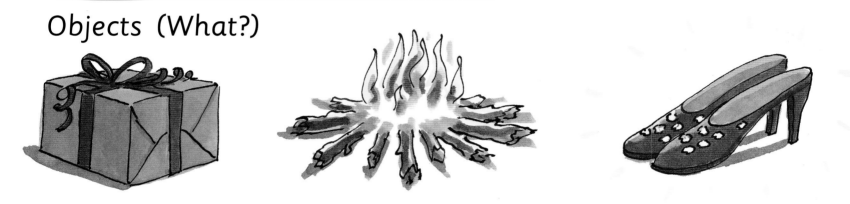

### Settings (Where?)

★ **Watch out!**

Choose a character and a setting. Take turns to warn each other about them.

○ **Don't** open the door, **because** there's a fiery dragon outside.

★ **Guess what!**

Make up a silly sentence linking a character, an object, and a setting.

○ **Guess what! There's a** strange alien sailing a boat on the river.

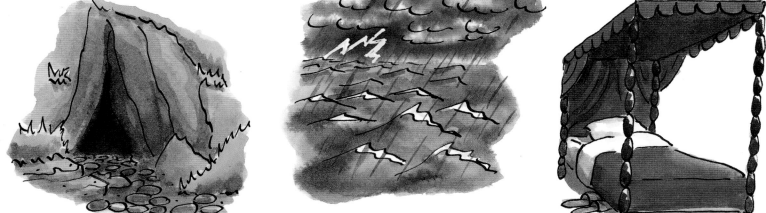

★ **Who goes there?**

Make up some sentences saying **who** went **where** with **what**.

◯ **The** witch **went** over the bridge **with** a present.

★ **Tell a tale**

Make up a story about two of the characters.

◯ One day, a dragon knocked at the door of a castle. A witch opened it. Angrily, she waved her wand and turned the dragon into a pile of bones.

# What's going on? Tell the story.

★ **Tell me**

Choose a picture. Say what's happening in it.

◯ There's a man crossing a bridge over a river. He's carrying a heavy load. The bridge is about to break. Hungry crocodiles are lurking.

★ **What will happen next?**

Choose a picture. Say what you think might happen next.

◯ The children go into the dark kitchen. They hear a scuffling noise. When they turn round, they...

★ **Imagine a conversation**

What might the people in each picture be saying
to one another?

🗨 The girl says, "Taste my cake."

🗨 The giant replies, "I'd rather taste YOU!"

★ **Tell the whole story**

Make up a whole story about one of the pictures.
Name the characters and say where the story
takes place.

🗨 Once there were two children called. . .

# A faraway land
## Make up a story.

✦ **Choose one or two of these characters.**
What are their names? Where do they live?
What are they like? Begin your story.

💬 **Once upon a time** there was/were...

✦ Imagine they live in the village. They decide
to go on a journey. Where will they go? What are
they going to do there? Which road do they take?

✦ On the way they meet another character.
Choose one of these.

✦ What does this person or animal say and do?
How do your characters react?

✦ What happens next?

✦ How and where does your story end?

# Extension activities

## Pages 6-7    Cliffs, sand, and sky

*This spread provides practice in hearing and using consonant blends at the start (e.g. **fl**ag), in the middle (e.g. ha**mp**er) and at the end (e.g. sa**nd**) of words.*

✦ Invent sentences which include several examples of the same consonant blend for the child to complete, e.g. Ha**nd** in ha**nd**, we walked along the… (sa**nd**).

✦ Play *I-spy*, choosing objects in the picture that begin (or end) with a particular consonant blend, e.g. **sk**.

## Pages 8-9    Colorful characters

*These two pages provide practice in using precise description.*

✦ Choose two characters side by side. Identify the similarities and differences between them—including gender, age, hair color and style, eye color, facial expression, clothing, accessories, and so on.

✦ Ask the child to describe a person in the room, or someone you know, in as much detail as possible.

✦ Ask the child to describe an imaginary character, e.g. a giant, a queen or a bear, including details about his or her looks, characteristics, and feelings.

## Pages 10-11    Monsters everywhere!

*This double page provides opportunities to use precise description about actions as well as appearances, and to use prepositions to describe location.*

✦ Play *Those monsters*. Take turns to describe what the monsters have done, adding a new sentence each time, e.g. **Those monsters** have messed up the bedroom. **Those monsters** have messed up the bedroom and jumped on the sofa, and so on.

✦ Play *Where's my purse?* Imagine you have hidden a purse somewhere in the monster house. Children have to ask precise questions to discover its whereabouts, e.g. Is it under a cushion? Is it behind the sofa?

## Pages 12-13    Princess Polly's birthday

*These pages provide further practice in description.*

✦ Play *Princess Polly's room*. Children think of action words (verbs) to describe Princess Polly and her room, e.g. Princess Polly **danced around** her room.

✦ Play *Arthur the king*. Take turns to think of an adjective to describe Arthur the king, perhaps choosing the adjectives in alphabetical order, e.g. Arthur is an **amazing** king; Arthur is a **bald** king; etc.

✦ Use the picture for making up stories. Imagine that the party is the starting point for an adventure or a celebration at the *end* of an adventure.

## Pages 14-15    Mix and match

*This double page is concerned with classifying and comparing objects.*

✦ Choose an object. Ask children to link it to as many other things in the picture as possible, giving reasons, e.g. The spade… is made of wood and metal like the ax and the saw, is used for digging like the trowel, has a handle like the mug and watering can, etc.

✦ Play *The memory game*. Look at the picture for a couple of minutes, identifying all the objects.  Cover the picture or shut the book and see how many things the children can remember. (If this is too difficult, play the game with separate pages first of all.)

✦ Invent matching games with real, everyday objects.

## Pages 16-17    Woof! Woof!

*This double page focuses on discrimination and categorization.*

✦ Choose either two spotted dogs or two brown dogs in the picture. Ask the child to identify as many similarities and differences between them as possible—such as the length of their tails and ears; whether or not they have a collar and what color it is; what they are doing, etc.

✦ Compare and contrast. Use your own collections of objects to play similar matching games. You could also use pictures on a theme cut from magazines.

## Pages 18-19   The Glitz Hotel

*The pictures provide opportunities for making comparisons, asking questions, and describing a sequence of events.*

✦ Ask children to identify the people who work in the hotel and talk about what they do.

✦ Use both pictures to ask children questions about what they might see, hear, or smell in the hotel.

✦ Using the incidents in the hotel, ask children to play *What happened when?* e.g. What happened when the... bathwater overflowed; the dog ran away?

## Pages 20-21   Monkey mischief

*This picture encourages children to talk in sentences including prepositions or comparatives, or to talk about a sequence of events. It can also be used for discussing mathematical concepts, e.g. counting, sorting, and size.*

✦ **How many monkeys are...** swinging? laughing? running? gray? sitting?

✦ **Which is...** the biggest monkey? the hairiest? holding the most bananas?

✦ **Can you find...** two monkeys with babies? two monkeys holding bananas in their left hands?

## Pages 22-23   At the park

*This spread encourages children to use the appropriate conventions and language for giving instructions and directions and making rules.*

✦ Play *Follow the directions.* Ask a child to stand in the center of a rug or a room. Give directions, such as: walk three steps to the left, step one pace backward, etc.

✦ Talk about how children might design (and draw) their own obstacle race and what instructions they would need for it.

✦ Discuss what rules you might need for your classroom or home.

## Pages 24-25   What did you see?

*The pictures on this double page can be used for imaginative sentence making, linking the characters, settings, and objects.*

✦ Use question words to flesh out each character, e.g. **Who** is this alien? **Where** does it come from? **What** does it look like? **Why** has it come here? **How** did it travel?  Encourage children to answer in whole

sentences and also to ask their own questions.

✦ Ask children to make up sentences that explain how a **character** is linked with a **setting** and an **object**. First use the examples in the book and then invent your own. You could base the sentences on traditional tales.

## Pages 26-27   What's going on?

*The pictures each show an ambiguous situation, which children can interpret in as many different imaginative ways as they like. These could also stimulate imaginary conversations between the characters in the pictures.*

✦ *Let's imagine.* Think of some other situations with alternative possible outcomes to talk about, such as: Let's imagine you find a huge egg under your bed; your dog runs into a strange, overgrown yard, etc.

✦ Jointly tell a story, taking turns to say a few sentences. End each turn with a cliffhanger that the next person resolves as part of his or her turn, e.g. One day, Annie made a cake for tea. She had just put in on a rack to cool, when there was a loud knock at the door. To her surprise it was...

## Pages 28-29   A faraway land

*The story map offers alternative characters, routes, and destinations for creating a variety of traditional tales.*

✦ Encourage children to bring characters alive by describing their appearance, characteristics, and actions, and to imagine conversations between them. Suggest the use of adjectives to evoke the settings.

✦ Use traditional story language to help children structure their stories, such as:

**Openings:** There was once... Long ago, there lived...
**Build-ups:** On their way... Early one morning...
**Problem:** All of a sudden... In an instant...
**Resolution:** So... When... As soon as...
**Ending:** In the end... At last... Finally...

✦ Once children understand the structure of this story map, encourage them to use it further as a basis for creating their own stories, using new characters, settings and incidents, or to recount family stories and anecdotes about funny things that have happened.

## When I speak, I need to:

- ★ Look at the person to whom I'm talking.

- ★ Make sure I say words clearly.

- ★ Speak loudly enough for everyone listening to hear me.

- ★ Ask questions if I don't understand.

- ★ Remember not to speak too fast.

- ★ Let other people join in and have a turn.

## When I listen, I need to:

- ★ Look at the person who is speaking.

- ★ Keep still.

- ★ Follow carefully what the speaker is saying.

- ★ Wait until a speaker has finished before speaking.

- ★ Ask about anything I don't understand.

- ★ Give a reply if someone asks a question.